Farah Sharida's work is rooted in her experiences of living in a desert. She is inspired by nature and the scenery, and has been living in the United Arab Emirates for last ten years. All illustrations in the book are from her original artworks and paintings.

This book is dedicated to my daughters, Ciarah, Celina, Celeste and our pet, Oggy.

Farah Sharida

DESERT TALES OF THE EMIRATES

AUSTIN MACAULEY PUBLISHERS™

LONDON * CAMBRIDGE * NEW YORK * SHARJAH

ISBN – 9789948786009 – (Paperback)
ISBN – 9789948787990 – (E-Book)

Application Number: MC-10-01-7001280
Age Classification: E

Printer Name: iPrint Global Ltd
Printer Address: Witchford, England

First Published 2023
AUSTIN MACAULEY PUBLISHERS FZE
Sharjah Publishing City
P.O Box [519201]
Sharjah, UAE
www.austinmacauley.ae
+971 655 95 202

I am extremely grateful to the leaders of the UAE especially the late President Sheikh Khalifa bin Zayed al-Nahyan of the United Arab Emirates peace be upon him and all those in authority for giving me the opportunity to make the UAE my second home. I cannot begin to express my thanks and appreciation to my husband and kids for their steadfast support and encouragement.

Let me tell you '*A Desert Tale*' around a fireside, as we sip a hot cup of Karak Chai, reminiscing about the past, celebrating the present and anticipating all the wonders to come.

Let me tell you a story about a place built on the hopes and dreams of a unique visionary leader, whose love extends well beyond his own people, to include all who share a deeply embedded desire to be better.

Let me tell you a story about a powerful robust creature combing through the boundless lands. This phenomenal creature plays a vital role in this nation's flourishing equestrian legacy and its growing cultural exchange with other like-minded nations that also put great value in these quadruped sidekicks.

Let me tell you a story of a land filled with many riches, hidden within a shield of never-ending subtle caressing dunes which hug the lands from end to end.

Let me tell you a story of a nation with dynamic and progressive leaders that empower their youth.

Let me tell you a story of the powerful four-legged vintage vehicles which roam these lands even till today, reminding all about the past trials.

Let me tell you a story when rough waters were no match for these floating sanctuaries.

Let me tell you a story of hands which worked tirelessly to uncover hidden gems encased in crusty shell creatures of the deep waters.

Let me tell you a story of a people deeply rooted in their religion, where their praises filled the skies throughout the days with melodious chanting from golden pinnacles.

Let me tell you a story of majestic winged guardians roaming the endless expanse of skies with a watchful eye.

Let me tell you a story of a gentle muscular beast prancing though this dusty land.

Let me tell you a story about the wise old flippered companion of the reefs.

Let me tell you a story about that slithering sneaky sly one who may catch you by surprise.

Let me tell you a story of a place where dazzling skylines grew out of the dust.

Let me tell you a story about the night sky filled with burst of colorful, fiery glow raining down and showering over all below with its shimmery powder of excitement.

Let me tell you a story of a place far east where the sunsets, go out in a blazing glowing glory, kissing all with its last warm touch of the day.

Let me tell you a story of a place where hard work and perseverance sprouts endless possibilities and prosperity for present and future generations of all.

Let me tell you a story about a place called the United Arab Emirates with a mosaic of people bonded by a shared desire to excel in every venture they attempt, shinning as brightly as the gleaming golden minaret.